GRAMERCY GREAT MASTERS

Camille Pissarro

Gramercy Books
New York • Avenel

Acknowledgments
The publishers would like to thank the museums for reproduction permission and in particular the **BRIDGEMAN ART LIBRARY** for their help in supplying the illustrations for the book.

British Museum, London: An Orchard.
Christie's, London: The Avenue, Sydenham; The Road at Osny; View of the Road; Plum Trees in Flower; Cours La Reine, Rouen; The Port at Le Havre; Sunrise at Rouen; The Tuilleries Gardens and the Louvre.
Collection Durand-Ruel: Mother and Child in a Garden; The Siesta.
Dr. H.C.E. Dreyfus Foundation, Kunstmuseum, Basel: The Gleaners.
Carnegie Institute, Museum of Art, Pittsburgh: Le Grand Pont, Rouen.
Private collections: The Cabbage Slopes, Pontoise; The Stream at Osny; The Flood at Eragny; Pont Neuf, Paris.
Courtauld Institute Gallery, London: Trees in a Field with a Village in the Background.
Louvre, Paris: Trees at Louveciennes.
Musée d'Orsay, Paris: The Tumbledown Cottage Near Osny; The Stagecoach at Louveciennes; Landscape, Pontoise; Hillside of Vesinet, Yvelines; The Approach to the Village of Voisins; The Road at Louveciennes; The Hillside at L'Hermitage; Landscape; Harvesting at Montfoucault; The Red Roofs; A Corner of the Garden at L'Hermitage; Woman in an Orchard; The Seine and the Louvre, Paris; Vegetable Gardens at L'Hermitage.
Musée des Beaux-Arts, Le Havre: Apple Trees and Poplars in the Setting Sun.
Boston Museum of Fine Arts: The Market at Pontoise; The Market at Gisors.
Dallas Museum of Fine Arts: Apple-Pickers.
Museum of Fine Arts, Rennes: Avenue de l'Opéra, Paris.
Pushkin Museum, Moscow: The Ploughed Field; Paris Street Scene; Avenue de l'Opéra, Paris.
National Gallery of Scotland, Edinburgh: The Banks of the Marne at Chennevières.
National Gallery, London: The Côte des Bœufs at Pontoise; Boulevard Montmartre at Night.
Stadtische Kunsthalle, Mannheim: View of Pontoise: Quai au Pothuis.
Fondazione Buhrle, Zurich: Female Peasant Carding Wool.
Palais de Tokyo, Paris: Woman Hanging Up the Wash.
Tate Gallery, London: The Pork Butcher; Self-Portrait.

This 1994 edition is published by Gramercy Books,
distributed by Outlet Book Company, Inc.
a Random House Company,
40 Engelhard Avenue
Avenel, New Jersey 07001

Printed and bound in Italy

8 7 6 5 4 3 2 1

Camille Pissarro
HIS LIFE AND WORKS

There is not one single painting or one particular subject that distinguishes Pissarro's work from that of the other Impressionists. He did no studies of water lilies, no ballerinas, no cabaret dancers, no picnics in the park. Rather, it is Pissarro's consistent and adaptable body of work that makes him a great master.

Pissarro was a man of the people. A humanitarian and political socialist, he admired the simple life of the peasant and idealized it in his paintings of the French country villages of Osny, Eragny, and Pontoise. Later in his life, Pissarro also painted urban landscapes, worlds of movement, of traffic and activity on the Avenue de l'Opéra and on the Boulevard Montmartre at night.

Pissarro was a painter who spoke more of nature than its people. His landscapes, rural and urban, are magnificent studies of balance, color, and vibrancy. He is remembered as an artist who not only helped found the Impressionist movement but embraced it, molded it, and adapted it to the changing world.

The writer Émile Zola once said that "Pissarro is an unknown artist, and probably no one will ever talk about him. . . . An austere and serious style, extreme respect for truth and fidelity, a harsh and determined will. . . . Pissarro is an artist that I like."

Zola was wrong about Pissarro's lack of fame. But he was correct in describing his tenacity, his search for truth in painting and in life. As a socialist who believed in the good will of people, as a heroic figure who was determined to overcome the obstacles that stood in his way, and as a painter who tried to convey to the world the essence, or impression, of a scene, Pissarro had no peer.

Pissarro, the father of Impressionist painting, was a friend, mentor, and confidante of Monet, Degas, Seurat, and Renoir.

A CAREER IN TRADE

Jacob Abraham Camille Pissarro was born in 1830 in St. Thomas, Virgin Islands. His parents were Jewish. Frédéric, his father, had immigrated to the Islands from Bordeaux in 1824. His mother, Rachel Pomie-Manzana, was a young widow when she met Frédéric. The Pissarros were middle-class merchants who did well in the colonial trade of the times. They were sufficiently affluent to send their teenaged son to boarding school in Passy, a suburb of Paris. From 1842 to 1847, Pissarro enjoyed the relative freedom of a boarding school student, and after graduation he returned home.

Pissarro had not yet become a painter. Indeed, there is no evidence that he even took brush to paper in these early days. When he returned to the Virgin Islands, he joined his parents and his brother Alfred in the family business. But by 1852 he had had enough of what he later called "the bourgeois life," and with a friend, the Danish painter Fritz Melbye, he traveled to exotic Caracas in Venezuela.

In Caracas, Pissarro began to paint—and what had begun as a young man's rebellion grew into a serious determination to become an artist. In October 1855, Pissarro renounced all ties to the family business and moved to Paris, the artistic capital of the world.

TRUE BEGINNINGS

Pissarro immediately enrolled in classes at the École des Beaux-Arts given by such academically reputable and approved neo-classical painters as Henri Lehmann and François Picot. He learned the fundamentals of art and, in the neoclassical tradition, the painting of studio-drawn narratives, the grand-scale

10

interpretations of history and mythology. But when Pissarro went to the World's Fair, which was held in Paris in 1855, he realized how much more there was to painting than re-creating and romanticizing classical lines and shapes.

At this famed exhibition, he saw the French Realist painter Gustave Courbet's *Pavillon du Realisme* and Jean-Baptiste Camille Corot's landscapes. Here was movement and color, a free, idyllic sense of harmony and lyricism in the bucolic countryside, in the skies and hills. Here were paintings of the times, full of life, of real people in real situations.

In France in the late nineteenth century, the burgeoning urban middle class was exerting a powerful influence on economics, politics, and social structure. In the lyrical landscape paintings exhibited at the World's Fair, they found a world of peace and harmony. They could identify with this art. It was familiar and desirable—a great contrast to the mythological, grand-scale representations of formal neoclassicism. And, even more crucial for the artists of the era, these people could afford to pay for their enthusiasms.

Pissarro was strongly influenced by Courbet's realistic style and Corot's landscape paintings. Their work helped him discover his own predilection for landscape art, and he even took some classes with Corot. In 1857, he spent the summer at Montmorency and began to paint outside, surrounded by nature's aura. His *Gardens and Trees in Flower* show Corot's influence, but Pissarro's unique style was already emerging. He was beginning to treat light with less massive depth. His shadings were lighter. *The Outskirts of Paris*, which he painted the same year, show that he was gravitating toward the movement and lightness of impressionistic art.

Corot, Théodore Rousseau, and Jean-François Millet were among the members of the Barbizon school, named for a village near the Fontainebleau forest. These artists concentrated on the French countryside. They painted their surroundings with classical and natural realism—but with a difference. The Barbizon school considered nature a refuge from the ills of the world, and their paintings depicted bucolic peaceful places, and simple rustic lives. They used brushstrokes creatively. This was particularly true of Rousseau. He used the brushstroke to bring depth to the trees, to illuminate the skies.

Pissarro also admired Courbet's Realism. He was not alone. Courbet influenced many of the young Impressionists with his unique use of the palette knife to create textures and form.

These innovative applications of paint in the work of the artists of the Barbizon school and of Courbet marked the beginnings of Impressionistic art.

FORGING FRIENDSHIPS

Pissarro's personal life was a study in contrasts. While he embraced rural life, he preferred to live in the city. Although he eschewed bourgeois values, he willingly accepted the stipend his parents sent him each month. But these contradictions were also evidence of his flexibility. The money, of course, gave him the opportunity to paint. Living in the city made it possible for him to study with the masters. It also gave him a chance to meet the artists, philosophers, and writers of the times.

For ten years Pissarro continued to study at the École des Beaux-Arts. But he spent his spare time at the more avant-garde Académie Suisse. Not only were free classes offered there, but it had become an important gathering place for artists whose sensibilities and ambitions lay outside the official schools of artistic thought. At the Académie Suisse, art and painting, philosophy and technique, were freely and openly discussed. The debates were lively and Pissarro was able to define his own philosophy of art, which was based on a spontaneous display of nature combined with subtle but carefully constructed composition. Here, at the Académie Suisse, Pissarro met Claude Monet, Pierre Auguste Renoir, Paul Cézanne, and others who would be instrumental in the Impressionist movement.

Pissarro's life also included Julie Vellay, who had worked as a maid for his parents. When Pissarro visited the Virgin Islands in 1860, they met and their love affair began, much to his parents' disapproval. Their snobbery further alienated Pissarro from his "bourgeois roots," and Julie soon moved to Paris and into his suburban apartment. In 1863, their first child, Lucien, was born.

THE TURNING POINT

In these early days of experimentation with technique and style, Pissarro's favorite subject was the French countryside. *The Tumbledown Cottage Near Osny*, *The Small Factory*, and *The Banks of the Marne* show his great capacity to bring to the canvas the robust reality of simple country life.

The year 1863 also marked a turning point in French painting, which had long been dominated by the Académie des Beaux-Arts. In France at that time paintings were exhibited only by the official Salon, whose members were made up of Academy professors and administrators; it was the only place where French artists could show their work. The number of submissions for each exhibition was enormous, but only those paintings consistent with the rigid, conservative views of the academics were ever displayed. In 1863, three thousand artists submitted five thousand paintings and only two thousand of these were accepted.

The rejected artists protested loudly enough for Napoleon III to decree that a second Salon should be allowed to display work alongside the official one. This Salon des Refusés included the exuberant, new work of the burgeoning Impressionists, the talented painters of the "here and now." There were paintings by Corot, Cézanne, Millet, and Courbet, as well as Édouard Manet's famous *Déjeuner sur l'Herbe*, with its scandalously naked picnicker enjoying an afternoon in the country. Here, too, were landscapes by Pissarro, displaying a balance between carefully delineated composition and spontaneous natural settings.

Unfortunately, the Salon des Refusés was a fiasco. Although these brave painters naively believed that the public was ready to enthusiastically embrace their new look at life, they were attacked by critics as well as the public. They were called "reprobates"—and worse. Undaunted, Pissarro and his colleagues continued to paint and to discuss their ideas. They would meet at the Brasserie des

Martyrs, at the Café Guerbois, and at the Académie Suisse, developing and reaffirming a style that did not yet appeal to the public.

Pissarro joined the Société des Aquafortistes in 1863 and began to create etchings on copper plates that he would later print. He also began to explore "symbolic realism" in his paintings, thus shedding the influence of Corot and Courbet by composing works that were more symbolic. Instead of realistic shading and perspective, Pissarro concentrated on the feeling imparted by his subject, the expression the landscape created in his mind's eye. In *The Jallais Coast*, for example, he used thick color, spread with a spatula, to create texture and symmetry. In *The Hillside at L'Hermitage*, the hill is compact and massive. The nearby houses are represented as distinct surfaces of light and shadow. The patterns of these surfaces are echoed in the hills themselves, giving the landscape a coherence from which the trees' leaves and branches do not detract. Yet, as carefully constructed as this picture is, the expressive, almost spontaneous feeling of the countryside is present.

Unfortunately, Pissarro's lack of commercial success resulted in a lack of funds. Even with the interest of the Parisian art dealer Père Martin, his work did not sell well. To support his family, which now included a daughter, Julie-Rachel, who was born in 1865, he painted stop signs and window blinds. In 1869, he moved his family to Louveciennes near Versailles.

The advent of the railroad made travel to and from Paris easy. Now Pissarro could live in his beloved countryside and still be exposed to the cultural and artistic sophistication he craved. The landscapes he painted in Louveciennes display his mastery of color and texture, and his ability to convey the mood and expression of rural village life. *View from Louveciennes*, *The Forecourt at Louveciennes*, *The Stagecoach at Louveciennes*, *Winter Landscape*, and *The Road at Louveciennes* are among the many paintings he did of the village. They are composed around its winding roads, which curve past trees and houses, farm workers and villagers.

During the months of 1869, Pissarro also began to intertwine these winding roads with reflections in water, adding depth to the scenes. His later works, *The Seine at Bougival* and *The Weir at*

Garden and Trees in Flower

The Small Bridge, Pontoise

Pontoise, for example, show his talent for creating perfectly balanced fluid compositions.

Pissarro's "winding, watery roads" are considered the best of all his paintings. Because Impressionists painted in the open air, these paintings are, by definition, limited to a single scene. But within each scene lies a universe of harmony and expression. The reflections in the water extend to the whole landscape, from houses and hills to trees and farm workers. Although the gray and brown tones so favored by Corot dominate the compositions, the shades have a fine precision. And there are hints of greens and violets.

Pissarro's use of the winding road was brilliant. While it turned and curved around village walls, across banks of trees, along the water's edge, it freed him from the rigidity of linear perspective. In his later painting *The Castle at Busagny, Osny*, for example, he concentrated on selected elements within the scope of the road and still remained faithful to nature.

To London

On July 17, 1870, the Franco-Prussian War broke out, and in December Pissarro was forced to abandon his studio in Louveciennes. He and his family, along with his good friend Monet, fled to London, which proved to be more than a refuge from the war. There, in the national galleries, Pissarro and Monet were introduced to the brilliance of James McNeill Whistler's watercolors and the magical, proto-Impressionistic landscapes of J.M.W. Turner and John Constable. In these great works of art, the French artists discovered the abstract forms that conjured up images, the loose applications of light and color that brought movement to the scenes, the celebration of nature in all its power that would influence them as well as the development of Impressionism.

In Pissarro's *Dulwich College, London* there is evidence of Constable's influence. Here the artist used a gray-brown palette to escape the rigidity of natural colors and harmony, creating a mood that perfectly conveyed what nature had wrought, without its formal rules of reality.

Pissarro also made a valuable contact during his London sojourn. He became quite friendly with the English art dealer Paul Durand-Ruel—who would later become a champion of Impressionism, as well as of Pissarro.

The war was brief. In 1871 Pissarro, recently married to Julie, was able to return with his family to Louveciennes. Unfortunately, the Prussians had demolished his studio. Fifteen hundred works of art were destroyed, and only forty left unharmed.

BACK HOME

By the time Pissarro's second son, Georges, was born in 1871, it was time to leave Louveciennes. In August, the family moved to Pontoise. Although Pissarro kept a studio in Paris, this rural village was his home for many years.

In these early years of the 1870s, Pissarro was friendly with Monet, the landscape artist Alfred Sisley, and Cézanne, who lived in the nearby town of Auvers-sur-Oise. They introduced each other to potential art dealers. They painted the same scenes. They shared the same studio space. As outcasts in the artistic world, they were also comrades-in-arms.

But there was a change in Pissarro when he returned to France. His style reflected much of Monet's inventiveness, including his small, rapid brushstrokes, his studied reflections shimmering in water, his use of outlines. Here, too, is his friend Monet's influence in the continuous movement of light and shadow in such paintings as *A Corner of the Garden at L'Hermitage* and *Harvesting at Montfoucault*. Pissarro, in turn, influenced his friend with the technical, harmonious restraint he used so well, a technical brake that helped make Monet's paintings more cohesive and complete.

Pissarro was also strongly influenced by the Turner and Constable paintings he had seen in London. This influence is evident in the fluid lines and luminous, subtle use of tone and color in such paintings as *Misty Morning at Creil* and one of his most significant works, *The Haystack*, which is a galaxy of colors, each distinct, each contributing to the creation of a light

Dulwich College,
London

The Castle at Busagny,
Osny

that invades everything: the pink, white, and violet sky, the plain, the almost conical haystack, even the scene's shadowy areas.

Pissarro painted and painted. As he later wrote to his son, Lucien, "I did my painting no matter where; in all seasons, in heat waves, rain, terrible cold, I found the means to work with enthusiasm."

He also worked with an important mission in mind: to convey his ideas, his thoughts, to others. In 1873, Pissarro completed his famous self-portrait, which shows him mature, solid, and white-haired. His figure is majestic and sensitive, monumental and loving. It implies the artist's profound desire to communicate with the world.

The Birth of the Impressionist Movement

As much as Pissarro and the other burgeoning Impressionists painted with enthusiasm and verve, they could not sell their style to the public. Paul Durand-Ruel, who had been their staunchest champion, could no longer find buyers for their paintings. Strong measures were needed, not only for the sake of the Impressionist movement, but for the financial survival of the artists.

In 1874, the challenge to the official Salon was put in motion when these friends who had been working together for years formed a group of independent artists. Pissarro, Manet, Monet, Degas, Renoir, and twenty-five others founded the Anonymous Society of Artists, Painters, Sculptors, and Engravers. The group had only one purpose in mind: to reach the buying public without going through the conservative academic jury of the official Salon.

Pissarro, whose political leanings were moving more and more to the left—and farther from his bourgeois roots—wanted the group to adapt his socialistic spirit of "one for all." Degas, fearing public outrage, tried to temper Pissarro's enthusiasm by including the work of painters whom the establishment favored. He wanted to make the exhibition more acceptable to the critics, the public, and the powerful Salon jury.

Degas was right to be concerned. When the first Impressionist exhibition opened in 1874 in a photographer's studio on the Boulevard des Capucines, the reaction was even more violent than the artists had expected. It was a disaster. There they were, 165 paintings from thirty artists (including Claude Monet's *Impression: Sunrise*, which gave the movement its name), hanging on walls of red velvet. And, although his more cautious friends advised against it, Pissarro daringly participated with five works.

People flocked to the exhibit, but they didn't buy, or they made such ridiculously low offers that it was humiliating. The exhibit was treated as a sideshow. In a disparaging way, a critic from the publication *Le Charivari* coined the name Impressionism from the Monet painting. Others joined him, ferocious in their attack. One critic wrote, "They take canvases, paints, and brushes, splash on a few colors haphazardly and sign their name to the whole."

But none of them realized the strength of these artists' beliefs. Instead of crumbling, they embraced the critic's definition and began planning a second Impressionist show. This one, in 1876, took place at Durand-Ruel's galleries, but it was no more successful than its predecessor.

By the third show, in May 1877, the group was officially calling their style Impressionism. But official or not, this show fared no better than the other two. The remaining five shows, given from 1879 to 1886, were all financial failures. It was difficult for the artists. They needed to earn a living; emotions were frayed from the struggle. Pissarro was no exception. He doggedly continued to paint his own way, even when his finances were strained to the limits as he tried to support his growing family.

Over the years, the struggle, the development, and the sheer passing of time played a role in changing Impressionism. Some of the artists dropped out. Monet wanted to make the exhibits more commercial—and profitable. Pissarro disagreed. He was an idealist, becoming more and more entrenched in the world of social utopias and anarchy. Although the public did not buy his rural celebrations of color, texture, and composition, including *Côte des*

Boeufs at Pontoise, his *L'Hermitage* series of landscapes, and his *Washhouse at Bougival*, he did not give up.

By the fourth show, in 1879, however, Monet and Renoir had become so established that they began exhibiting work in the official Salon. Impressionism was beginning to become accepted by the public. And with this mainstream acceptance, the artistic fervor was lost. It needed a new direction.

By the early 1880s, Degas also became one of the many Impressionist artists who rejected the movement he helped found. He became one of the growing number of Post-Impressionists, those artists who needed to go beyond the limitations set by nature. Degas had always preferred an artificial setting between artist and model. Now, newer and younger artists joined him, including Mary Cassatt, Paul Gauguin, Vincent van Gogh, and Georges Seurat.

Gauguin, who had studied with Pissarro in Pontoise in 1881, composed more abstract canvases. His compositions did not rely on the usual rules of perspective. Vincent van Gogh created swirls of colors that would not normally belong in the environment he painted; vivid oranges and reds for bedrooms, blues and startling yellows for fields. Georges Seurat developed his pointillist technique, dissecting the natural light used in Impressionism into a modern formula of color theory. He applied paint in minute dots that blended together when a viewer gazed at it. The result was composition that was far more static than the spontaneous foundation of Impression. His *A Sunday on La Grande Jatte*, exhibited in the last Impressionist show in 1886, created a sensation. No one had seen anything like pointillism before. While Renoir, Monet, and Cézanne refused to exhibit next to Seurat's paintings, Pissarro was completely taken by him. He saw pointillism as an answer to the fleeting quality of Impressionist art.

This was the magic of Pissarro, embracing the new, experimenting with it, and integrating it. From Courbet and Monet, and Cézanne and Seurat, Pissarro took some color from here, a brushstroke from there, to create his own style and masterpieces.

Indeed, during the twelve-year span between the eight Impressionist exhibits, he painted some of his greatest works of art.

MASTERPIECES OF RURAL LIFE

In 1875, Pissarro was living in poverty. He had attempted more commercially accessible engravings, pastels, watercolors, and temperas, with limited success. Critics continued to call his paintings "unfinished." Then Théodore Duret, an art critic and friend, suggested he pay more attention to the human figure to make his canvases more visually stimulating. This led to a shift in style, culminating in a series of major paintings.

Female Peasant Pushing a Wheelbarrow and *Young Girl in a Garden* both depict simple and modest scenes, but the luminous colors alone are capable of transporting a viewer into the land of fables. *The Railway Bridge, Pontoise* avoids any suggestion of the cliché-ridden "picturesque." Here, Pissarro evokes an ideal, pure structure that blends perfectly with its surrounding natural setting. Everything in the picture implies freedom and peace. He seems to propose a vision of nature freed from restraints.

In 1877, Pissarro began to use fast, erratic brushstrokes. His paintings were no longer contemplative and passive. Instead, these new strokes and his vivid use of color evoked the dazzling light of the sun. In his famous *Red Roofs* Pissarro creates a unique vibration, a movement achieved through the rapid succession of lights and shadows. Here, through the seemingly moving branches of the trees, are the houses, a counterpoint to the landscape, providing both a mysterious element and a fusion of shape to the canvas.

By 1880, Pissarro finally had achieved a modicum of success. His attention almost completely shifted to human figures. The natural landscapes of the past decade became active, fluid scenes of peasant life. Here were harvesters and wool carders, market-stall hawkers and butchers, apple-pickers and clothes washers, shepherds and water-carriers, farmers' wives and children resting from their daily work.

This new subject matter coincided with Pissarro's increasingly

*The Forecourt
of Louveciennes*
(detail)

socialistic views. He had begun reading *Le Proletaire*, a socialist newspaper, as well as the revolutionary works of Zola and Flaubert. He believed in the goodness of humankind, brought to the fore through a return to the soil, to simple work and rustic communal living.

The Shepherdess, painted in 1881, is one of Pissarro's first paintings where the human figure plays the pivotal role. His small brushstrokes and occasionally intense colors create a rigorous composition. At the same time, the young woman's pose, the shadows and colors of her form, convey a tinge of melancholy, which is reinforced by an almost abstract background. *The Shepherdess* influenced the fledgling Gauguin, whose later portraits were painted against a neutral backdrop.

The Market at Gisors teems with life. The carefully composed figures create a natural rhythm, a movement that is reflected in the use of light, sharp brushstrokes in the trees above their heads. Here, too, is carefully placed detail: in the chickens in the foreground, in the child petting a dog near the center, in the calculated use of greens and blues.

Pissarro's *Road with a View of Epulches* of 1881 foreshadows his later infatuation with Seurat's pointillism. The painting concentrates on systematic, almost rigid, techniques, which compromised the usual happy equilibrium between spontaneity and symmetry that marked his style. Indeed, when Pissarro was introduced to Seurat in 1885, he was ready for a more scientific approach to art.

A BRIEF TIME WITH POINTILLISM

Seurat's new "dot" technique seemed a godsend to Pissarro, who, at the time, was searching for a new way to create natural light. He wanted the abstract elements of his style—the backgrounds, the lighting cast on the figures, the composition itself—made visible. He wanted not only to depict rural life, but to glorify it, to bestow on it a deeper, intellectual quality that would provide dignity and grace.

Pissarro found his answers in pointillism. To the astonishment and disapproval of his Impressionist friends, he turned to Seurat's "dots" in a series of paintings of rural life.

Pissarro searched for landscapes with wide horizons because they lent themselves to this new technique. *La Maison de la Sourde* and *The Bell-Tower at Eragny*, the canvas that came closest to Seurat's style, offers a sweeping view of Eragny, the small village to which Pissarro and his family had moved in 1884. Here, light covers every element, like tiny pearls, giving a fairy-tale effect.

View from My Window, Eragny, painted in 1888, reflects the ordered perfection he felt was found in rural, agricultural life. The dot technique is controlled and precise. The composition is a study of strong horizontals and verticals.

The Gleaners (1888) is speckled with dots of white. Combined with the rolling hills, the solidity of the figures, and the symmetry of the overall design, the painting is imbued with perfect dignity and grace.

As masterful as these works of art were, they were ultimately replaced with a looser, easier style. Pissarro began to feel cramped by the dot technique. It began to hamper his true spirit, his need for creative variety and vitality. The necessary slowness of the method, the very principles of color analysis that motivated it, were in direct contrast with his own vibrant, free vision. His canvases were in danger of becoming mechanical. As one critic wrote, Pissarro was ready to find a new solution to the problem of "fixing the impression of a dominant that is broken, served, and contested by reflections and the complementaries."

The ongoing search for this solution was hampered when, in 1888, Pissarro got an eye infection that would plague him for the rest of his life. Because of the infection, he was no longer able to stay outdoors for long periods of time. He had to paint the world from his windows.

ACCLAIM IN LATER LIFE

In 1890, Pissarro had his first one-man exhibition at Théo van Gogh's galleries. It was his first critical and commercial success,

The Railway Bridge,
Pontoise (detail)

enabling him to travel briefly to London to visit his son Lucien, now a painter, who had settled there. During this visit, he dropped pointillism completely and reverted to his old style of natural spontaneity combined with a lyrical, balanced composition.

Although he did experiment with moralistic Pre-Raphaelite realism in *Female Peasant Dreaming, Sunset*, and *The Female Cowherd*, he quickly realized that the flat, medieval brushstroke was not for him. *Serpentine, Hyde Park—The Effects of the Fog* illuminates his permanent return to Impressionism. The painting exquisitely portrays its subject without any geometrical constrictions. Despite the swirls of fog, the picture is complete and natural.

Woman with a Green Shawl, painted in 1893, is also a perfect Impressionist work. Light and shadow marvelously mingle, giving an exquisite grace to the subject.

Pissarro returned to Paris on a positive note. He had found a new solution for perfecting his art. He turned to the city in 1893, in a series of paintings depicting the life of Paris, Rouen, Dieppe, and Le Havre. Moving from hotel to hotel, from the Hôtel Garnier in Paris to the Hôtel de Paris in Rouen and places in between, he set up his canvas by the window and painted. He began several works at once, putting one aside for another if the weather changed, the traffic shifted, the light moved, or his mood altered. The wide boulevards and the sensuous Seine are captured forever in such great and successful works as the almost abstract *Boulevard Montmartre at Night*, the teeming *Paris Street Scene*, with its shimmering light and bold brushstrokes, *Avenue de l'Opéra*, and *The Seine and the Louvre, Paris*. *The Port at Le Havre* captures the essence of the location with its reflecting water, its waiting boats, and its massive sky. Thick brushstrokes evoke the scene of *Low Tide at Duquesne, Dieppe*. Tones of brown and gold subtly recreate a wakening city in *Sunrise at Rouen*

Although he painted this masterful series from his window, the viewer is never brought inside, nor made aware of the artist or the borders of his window frame. Rather, these paintings have the same freedom and expansiveness of Pissarro's earlier rural works.

*The Seine
at Bougival*

*Low Tide at Duquesne,
Dieppe*

They provide a perfect balance between symmetry, naturalism, and spirit.

Pissarro's city series consumed the last ten years of his life. While he was working on these masterpieces, he also had his first retrospective in 1894, exhibiting 122 works at Duran-Ruel's galleries. After years of financial hardship and invisibility, the public was ready to embrace him. Art dealers actually began to vie for his canvases. His work was exhibited in Europe and overseas, in Pittsburgh and Boston.

But despite the security of his huge success, Pissarro turned down a commission for genre work. He did not want to be constricted by marketing concerns. He would rather paint his much-loved views, his enchanting images of flowers, his essence of city and rural life.

In November 1903, Pissarro was taken ill at the Hôtel du Quai Voltaire in Paris. He died in the hospital on November 13 and was buried in the Cemetery of Père-Lachaise in Paris.

Camille Pissarro was an Impressionist in the most complete sense of the term. He spent his life searching for ways to express the light around him. He was never afraid to become his pupils' pupil to enrich his own artistic language. He helped spread the ideals and style of Impressionism throughout the world.

Near the end of his life, he said, "Everyone . . . must paint according to their own vision." Indeed, Pissarro lived, worked, painted, and dreamed according to his own vision—and it is this vision that makes him a truly great master.

Young Girl in a Garden

HIS WORKS

The Tumbledown Cottage Near Osny

The Banks of the Marne at Chennevières

View of Pontoise: Quai au Pothuis

Trees at Louveciennes

The Stagecoach at Louveciennes

Winter Landscape

The Avenue, Sydenham

Hillside of Vesinet, Yvelines

The Approach to the Village of Voisins

The Road at Osny

The Road at Louveciennes

View of the Road

The Hillside at L'Hermitage

The Ploughed Field

Female Peasant Carding Wool

Landscape, Pontoise

Harvesting at Montfoucault

The Red Roofs

The Côte des Bœufs at Pontoise

A Corner of the Garden at L'Hermitage

Vegetable Gardens at L'Hermitage

The Cabbage Slopes, Pontoise

The Stream at Osny

The Pork Butcher

The Market at Gisors

Mother and Child in a Garden

Woman in an Orchard

Woman Hanging Up the Wash

The Market at Pontoise

Apple-Pickers

Plum Trees in Flower

The Gleaners

An Orchard

Cours La Reine, Rouen

Avenue de l'Opéra, Paris

Boulevard Montmartre at Night

The Flood at Eragny

The Port at Le Havre

Le Grand Pont, Rouen

Paris Street Scene

Avenue de l'Opéra, Paris

Sunrise at Rouen

The Siesta

The Tuilleries Gardens and the Louvre

Apple Trees and Poplars in the Setting Sun

Trees in a Field with a Village in the Background

Pont Neuf, Paris

The Seine and the Louvre, Paris

Self-Portrait

Stampa Grafiche Editoriali Padane Cremona